Guideposts *Prayers for Christmas*

Guideposts®

Prayers

FOR
CHRISTMAS

Compiled by Julie K. Hogan

Almighty God, when You came to us,
a darkened world was struck by light,
not only at Christmas but for all eternity.
How can we ever thank You enough?
—*Norman Vincent Peale*

IDEALS PUBLICATIONS, A DIVISION OF GUIDEPOSTS
NASHVILLE, TN

ISBN 0-8249-4601-4

Published by Ideals Publications, a division of Guideposts

535 Metroplex Drive, Suite 250
Nashville, Tennessee 37211
www.idealspublications.com

Caseside printed in the U.S.A. Text printed and bound in Mexico.
Printed by R.R. Donnelley & Sons.

Library of Congress Cataloging-in-Publication Data on file.

Publisher, Patricia A. Pingry
Art Director, Eve DeGrie
Research Assistant, Mary P. Dunn
Copy Editor, Amy Johnson
Editorial Assistant, Patsy Jay
Designed by DeGrie, Kennedy & Associates

ACKNOWLEDGMENTS

HOAGLAND, FATHER VICTOR. "Come Save Your People" and "Speak to My Heart." Used
by permission of Passionist Publications. http://cptryon.org/prayer/adx/index.html.
HYCLAK, FATHER WALLY. "Light of the World." Reprinted with permission of the
author. ICAZA-WILLETTS, LIA. "Bless Our Home." From www.gbod.org/family/arti-
cles/prayer.html. JOHN XXIII, POPE. "Child of Bethlehem." Translated by Dorothy
White. From *The Doubleday Prayer Collection*. Printed in 1997 by special arrangement with
Lion Publishing. Selected and arranged by Mary Batchelor. MARSHALL, PETER. "Give
Us the Faith" from *The Best of Peter Marshall*. Copyright © 1983 by Catherine Marshall
LeSourd. Published by Chosen Books. "Renaissance of Faith" from *Mr. Jones, Meet the
Master*. Copyright © 1949, 1950 by Fleming H. Revell Company. Reprinted with per-
mission of Baker Book House. "Wilt Thou Help Us" from *The Prayers of Peter Marshall*.
Published by McGraw-Hill Book Company. Copyright © 1959 by Catherine Marshall.
NOYES, MORGAN PHELPS. "The Peace of Christ" from *Prayers for Services*. Copyright ©
1954 by Charles Scribners' Sons. SUTER, JOHN W. "Send the Light" from *Prayers for a
New World*. Copyright © 1964 by Charles Scribners' Sons. Our sincere thanks to the fol-
lowing authors whom we were unable to locate: Jane Merchant for "A Prayer"; H. B.
Milward for "For This Day."

CONTENTS *Prayers for Christmas*

PRAYERS OF PREPARATION

Prepare ye the way of the Lord, make straight in the desert a highway for our God. Every valley shall be exalted, and every mountain and hill shall be made low: and the crooked shall be made straight, and the rough places plain: And the glory of the Lord shall be revealed, and all flesh shall see it together: for the mouth of the Lord hath spoken it. — Isaiah 40:3-5

PRAYERS OF PREPARATION

Speak to My Heart

O Jesus,
your voice sounds through the
house of my world:
"Be on your guard! Stay awake!"
Yet I hardly hear you.
Busy with so much, I go about the things
I do like a servant trapped
in household routine,
hardly giving a thought
to what my life is about.
My spirit within has grown tired
and you, my God, seem far away.
How can I hear your voice today?
Speak to my heart
during this season of grace,
as you spoke to your prophets and saints.
Remind me again of the journey
you call me to make and the work
you would have me do.

I am your servant, O Lord.
Speak to me in this holy season
and turn my eyes
to watch for your coming.
O Emmanuel, Jesus Christ,
desire of every nation,
Savior of all peoples,
come and dwell among us.

—Attr. to Father Victor Hoagland

Come Save Your People

O Jesus,
in an empty desert
your prophet John proclaimed:
God is here, at your side.
God has come to bring about a kingdom
where injustice and suffering
will be no more, where tears
will be wiped away,
and where those who turn to God
will feast at a banquet.

"Turn now, your God
is standing at your side.
Reform your lives,
God's kingdom is at hand."
In an empty desert John said these things.

Give me faith like John's, O Lord,
strong enough to believe
even in a desert
that you and your kingdom
are no farther from me
than my hand.
Make my heart strong like his,
not swayed by trials
or snared by false pleasures.
Give me courage to be faithful
until your promises are fulfilled.
O King of all nations, Jesus Christ,
only joy of every heart,
come and save your people.

—*Attr. to Father Victor Hoagland*

Stir Up Our Hearts

Stir up our hearts, we beseech you,
to prepare ourselves
to receive your Son.
When he comes and knocks,
may he find us not sleeping in sin,
but awake to righteousness,
ceaselessly rejoicing in his love.
May our hearts and minds
be so purified,
that we may be ready to receive
his promise of eternal life.

— *The Gelasian Sacramentary*

The Incarnation

O God,
who looked on us
when we had fallen down into death,
and resolved to redeem us
by the Advent of your only begotten Son;
grant, we beg you,
that those who confess
his glorious Incarnation
may also be admitted to the fellowship
of their Redeemer,
through the same Jesus Christ
our Lord.

—*Saint Ambrose*

More Like Thee

O Lord,

give us more charity,

more self-denial,

more likeness to thee.

Teach us to sacrifice

our comforts to others,

and our likings for the sake of doing good.

Make us kindly in thought,

gentle in word,

generous in deed.

Teach us that it is better

to give than to receive,

better to forget ourselves

than to put ourselves forward,

better to minister than to be ministered unto.

And to thee, the God of love,

be all glory and praise, now and forever.

– Henry Alford

Incline Us, O God

Incline us, O God!
to think humbly of ourselves,
to be saved
only in the examination
of our own conduct,
to consider our fellow-creatures
with kindness,
and to judge of all they say and do
with the charity
which we would desire
from them ourselves.

— Jane Austen

Almighty God

Almighty God,

give us grace

that we may cast away the works of darkness,

and put upon us the armour of light,

now in the time of this mortal life,

in which thy Son Jesus Christ came

to visit us in great humility;

that in the last day,

when he shall come again in his glorious majesty

to judge both the quick and the dead,

we may rise to the life immortal,

through him who liveth

and reigneth with thee

and the Holy Ghost,

now and ever. Amen.

— From The Book of Common Prayer

The Lamb of God

May the Lamb of God,
who once came
to take away the sins of the world,
take away from us every stain of sin.
Amen.
And may he
who came to redeem what was lost,
at his second coming not cast away
what he has redeemed.
Amen.
That, when he comes,
we may have perpetual joy with him
on whom we have believed.
Amen.

— *From Mozarabic Breviary*

A Steadfast Heart

Give us, O Lord,
a steadfast heart,
which no unworthy affection
may drag down;
give us an unconquered heart,
which no tribulation
can wear out;
give us an upright heart,
which no unworthy purpose
may tempt aside.
Bestow upon us also,
O Lord our God,
understanding to know Thee,
diligence to seek Thee,
wisdom to find Thee,
and a faithfulness
that may finally embrace Thee,
even through Jesus Christ our Lord.

— *Thomas Aquinas*

Moonless Darkness

Moonless darkness
stands between.
Past, O Past, no more be seen!
But the Bethlehem star may lead me
To the sight of Him who freed me
From the self that I have been.

Make me pure, Lord:
Thou art holy;
Make me meek, Lord:
Thou wert lowly;
Now beginning, and alway:
Now begin, on Christmas Day.

— *Gerard Manley Hopkins*

Behold Your Gift

O Lord,
in this season
when our senses
are filled with "Jingle Bells"
and "Silent Night,"
friends and family,
and bowls of nuts and popcorn
around the Christmas tree,
when our spirits ache
and strain for release
through choir and organ
and candlelight,
surprise us anew
as we turn from all this
to behold Your Gift, Jesus,
One-on-one.

— *Author Unknown*

Dear Lord and Father

Dear Lord and Father of mankind,
Forgive our foolish ways!
Reclothe us in our rightful mind,
In purer lives Thy service find,
In deeper reverence, praise.

Drop Thy still dews of quietness,
Till all our strivings cease;
Take from our souls
The strain and stress,
And let our ordered lives confess
The beauty of Thy peace.

— John Greenleaf Whittier

Prepare Our Hearts

Father,

Prepare our hearts for Your coming.

Quiet the stirrings within.

Calm the busyness without.

Renew us with Your Spirit.

We are ready, Lord—

ready for Christmas . . .

Ready to hear

the cries of our injured neighbor.

Ready to extend

our hands to a fallen brother.

Ready to sit with a hurting friend.

Ready to comfort a grieving child.

Ready for You.

With open hearts,

we receive the Christ Child

into our lives today.

Amen.

— *Terri Castillo*

Open My Heart

Dearest God,
please never let me
crowd my life
full to the brim
so that, like the keeper
of Bethlehem's inn,
I find I have no room
for Him.
Instead, let my heart's door
be ever open,
ready to welcome
the newborn King.
Let me offer the best that I have
to Him who gives me
everything.

— *Rosalyn Hart Finch*

PRAYERS OF INVITATION

Therefore the Lord himself shall give you a sign;
Behold, a virgin shall conceive, and bear a son,
and shall call his name Immanuel. — Isaiah 7:14

O Long-Expected Jesus

Come, O long-expected Jesus,
Born to set your people free;
From our fears and sins release us;
Free us from captivity.

Israel's strength and consolation,
You, the hope of all the earth,
Dear desire of ev'ry nation,
Come, and save us by your birth.
Born your people to deliver;
Born a child, and yet a King!
Born to reign in us forever,
Now your gracious kingdom bring.

By your own eternal Spirit
Rule in all our hearts alone;
By your all-sufficient merit
Raise us to your glorious throne.

— *Charles Wesley*

Tarry Not

Come, Lord, and tarry not!
Bring the long-looked-for day!
O why these years of waiting here,
These ages of delay?

Come, for creation groans,
Impatient of your stay,
Worn out with these long years of ill,
These ages of delay.

Come, and make all things new,
Build up this ruined earth;
Restore our faded paradise,
Creation's second birth.

Come, and begin your reign
Of everlasting peace;
Come, take the kingdom to yourself,
Great King of righteousness!

— *Attr. to Horatius Bonar*

Come, Lord Jesus

O Wisdom,
which camest out of the mouth
of the Most High,
and reachest from one end of earth to another,
mightily and sweetly
ordering all things:
come and teach us
the way of prudence.
Even so, come Lord Jesus.

O Adonai,
and leader of the house of Israel,
who appearedst in the bush to Moses
in a flame of fire,
and gavest him the law on Sinai:
come and redeem us
with an outstretched arm.
Even so, come Lord Jesus.

O Root of Jesse,
which standest for an ensign to the people,
at whom kings shall shut their mouths,

whom the Gentiles shall seek:
come and deliver us, and tarry not.
Even so, come Lord Jesus.

O Day spring,
brightness of the light everlasting,
and Sun of righteousness:
come and enlighten them that sit
in darkness and the shadow of death.
Even so, come Lord Jesus.

O King of nations, and their desire;
the cornerstone, who makest both one:
come and save mankind,
whom thou formedst of clay.
Even so, come Lord Jesus.

O Emmanuel, our King and Lawgiver,
the desire of all nations and their salvation:
come and save us, O Lord our God.
Even so, come Lord Jesus.

—Author Unknown

O Lord Jesu Christ

O Lord Jesu Christ,
who at Thy first Coming
didst send Thy messenger
to prepare Thy way before Thee;
Grant that the ministers and stewards
of Thy mysteries may likewise so prepare
and make ready Thy way,
by turning the hearts of the disobedient
to the wisdom of the just,
that at Thy second Coming
to judge the world
we may be found an acceptable people in Thy sight,
Who livest and reignest with the Father
and the Holy Spirit,
ever one God,
world without end.
Amen.

— *Attr. to John Cosin*

Christmas Dedication

Lord Jesus,

I give you my hands to do your work,

I give you my feet to go your way,

I give you my eyes to see as you do.

I give you my tongue to speak your words,

I give you my mind that you may think in me,

I give you my spirit that you may pray in me.

Above all, I give you my heart

that you may love in me.

I give you my whole self

that you may grow in me,

so that it is you, Lord Jesus,

who live and work and pray in me.

I hand over to your care, Lord,

my soul and body, my mind and thoughts,

my prayers and hopes, my health and my work,

my life and my death,

my parents and my family,

my friends and my neighbours,

my country and all men. Today and always.

— *Lancelot Andrewes*

At Christmas

Good Jesu, born as at this time,
A little child for love of us;
Be thou born in me, that I may
Be a little child in love of thee;
And hang on thy love as on my
Mother's bosom,
Trustfully, lovingly, peacefully;
Hushing all my cares in love of thee.

Good Jesu, sweeten every thought of mine
With the sweetness of thy love.
Good Jesu, give me a deep love for thee,
That nothing may be too hard for me
To bear for love of thee.

— *E.B. Pusey*

Give Us, O God

Give us, O God,

the vision

which can see

Thy love in the world

in spite of human failure.

Give us the faith

to trust Thy goodness

in spite of our ignorance and weakness.

Give us the knowledge

that we may continue

to pray with understanding hearts,

and show us

what each one of us can do

to set forward the coming

of the day of universal peace.

— *Frank Borman*

Thy Kingdom Come

Thou hope of all the lowly!
　To thirsting souls how kind!
Gracious to all who seek Thee,
　Oh, what to those who find!

My tongue but lisps Thy praises,
　Yet praise me my employ;
Love makes me bold to praise Thee,
　For Thou art all my joy.

In Thee my soul delighting,
　Findeth her only rest;
And so in Thee confiding,
　May all the world be blest!

Dwell with us, and our darkness
　Will flee before Thy light;
Scatter the world's deep midnight,
　And fill it with delight.

O all mankind! behold Him
And seek His love to know;
And let your hearts, in seeking,
   Be fired with love and glow!
O come, O come, great Monarch,
   Eternal glory Thine;
The longing world waits for Thee!
   Arise, arise and shine!

—*Bernard of Clairvaux*

O Holy Child

O holy Child of Bethlehem,
Descend to us, we pray;
Cast out our sin, and enter in:
Be born in us today.
We hear the Christmas angels
The great glad tidings tell:
O come to us, abide with us,
Our Lord Emmanuel.

— *Phillips Brooks*

Come and Dwell

Lord Jesus Christ,
come and dwell in our hearts
this Christmastide,
so that our home may have you in it
and be full of joy and peace.
May no ill temper, impatience,
envy, or jealousy spoil the gladness
of your birthday,
but may love shine in our midst,
bringing light
to all our hearts and minds.

— *J. McDougall Ferguson*

PRAYERS OF FAITH

And it came to pass, as the angels were gone away from them into heaven, the shepherds said one to another, Let us now go even unto Bethlehem, and see this thing which is come to pass, which the Lord hath made known unto us. And they came with haste, and found Mary, and Joseph, and the babe lying in a manger. — Luke 2:15-16

We Give Thee Thanks

Our Heavenly Father,
let this message of Christmas
come into our hearts and minds.
We are not alone here,
either as individuals or as a human race.
Thou art with us,
help us to be with Thee.
Give us faith in the everlasting Saviour,
Jesus Christ, to save us individually
and as a people,
through the everlasting God,
the Prince of Peace,
the Saviour of mankind.
For this happiest news ever given,
we give Thee thanks.
Amen.

— *Norman Vincent Peale*

My Beloved Star

O my beloved Star,
so fascinate me
that I may not withdraw from Your radiance.

O consuming Fire,
Spirit of Love,
"come upon me,"
and create in my soul
an incarnation of your Word.

—*Elizabeth of the Trinity*

Prayer at the Manger

O God, whose mighty Son
was born in Bethlehem
those days long ago,
lead us to that same poor place,
where Mary laid her tiny Child.
And as we look on in wonder and praise,
make us welcome him in all new life,
see him in the poor,
and care for his handiwork:
the earth, the sky, and the sea.
O God, bless us again in your great love.
We pray for this through Christ our Lord.
Amen.

— Author Unknown

Let Your Goodness

Let your goodness, Lord,

appear to us,

that we, made in your image,

conform ourselves to it.

In our own strength we cannot imitate

your majesty, power, and wonder;

nor is it fitting for us to try.

But your mercy reaches from the heavens,

through the clouds, to the earth below.

You have come to us as a small child,

but you have brought us

the greatest of all gifts, the gift of eternal love.

Caress us with your tiny hands,

embrace us with your tiny arms,

and pierce our hearts with your soft, sweet cries.

— *Bernard of Clairvaux*

Our Heavenly Father

Our Heavenly Father,
we ask Thy blessing upon us all
and help us to find Jesus Christ,
really to find Him, not as an idea,
not as a theological concept,
not as a vague religious formula,
but as a warm, sweet, living Person,
with all His power
and life-changing force.
Then new life will be born again
in each of us.
O Lord,
let the same glory and wonderment
we had as little children
abide forever within us
through Jesus Christ, Our Lord,
Amen.

— *Norman Vincent Peale*

Help Us Understand

Our Heavenly Father,
help us to understand
that Christmas,
whatever other beauties it may have
and does have,
is the rebirth of Jesus Christ
in our lives. Amen.

— *Norman Vincent Peale*

Give Us the Faith

God of our fathers and our God,
give us the faith
to believe in the ultimate triumph
of righteousness . . .
We pray for the bifocals of faith
that see the despair
and the need of the hour
but also see, further on,
the patience of our God
working out His plan
in the world He has made.
In Thy sovereign name we pray,
Amen.

— *Peter Marshall*

Christmas Day Prayer

O God, my Father,
looking up at the shining stars
of the cold December sky
I remember the patient mother
and the rock-hewn manger
in lowly Bethlehem where lay cradled
Thy Love for the world.
In the shadows of the silent stall
I stand beside the Christ.
Speak to my soul as I wait, I pray Thee.
Let the trusting, loving spirit of the Child
steal into my life until it calms
my fears and soothes my pain.
In willing surrender and passionate longing
let me take the Christchild to my heart,
that henceforth I may live as He lived,
love as He loved, and, following His footsteps,
bring help to the needy, courage to the weak,
comfort to the sorrowing, and hope to the lost.
Amen.

— Author Unknown

Send Out Thy Light

Almighty and most merciful God,
toward whose everlasting blessedness
we ascend by the strong desire of the soul
and by patient continuance in well-doing;
lead us by thine inspiration
to seek our true life with thee
and earnestly to strive
to enter thy heavenly kingdom.
Send out thy light and thy truth:
let them lead us.
Set us free from the bondage
of self-will and passion
and ungodly desire,
that sin may not have dominion over us
but that with a willing mind
we may serve thee,
the Lord of heaven and earth.
Sanctify and renew us in the spirit of our minds.
Amen.

— Author Unknown

O Gifts of Gifts

O gifts of gifts! O grace of faith!
  My God! how can it be
That Thou, Who hast discerning love,
  Shouldst give that gift to me?

— *Frederick W. Faber*

Great King

Great King,

from heaven's high throne descending low,

In Bethlehem's stable born in cold and woe,

Thou shiverest in a manger, Babe Divine,

Much hast Thou borne for sin: how much for mine!

— *Saint Alphonsus Liguori*

The Accepting Heart

Holy Lord,
as taxpayers jostled through the streets
and filled the inns of the
busy clamorous town,
You came so quietly
to a dark, hidden, humble stable,
Your birth acknowledged on earth
by only a few shepherds.
Now millions celebrate Your birthday
with sound and light and lavish trappings.
Yet You still receive us
in a place as intimate as that hidden stable:
the accepting heart.
Come, Lord Jesus.

— *Norman Vincent Peale*

The Manger Prayer

There in the narrow manger bleak and cold
My Lord Thou art;
And there within those Hands, so soft and weak,
I lay my heart.
Beneath those tiny Feet I bow my head,
O blessed Child;
And kiss the straw that forms Thy chilly bed
In winter wild.

Upon Thy fair and youthful face I read
A look of love—
A look which bids me trust Thee in my need,
Spouse of the Dove.
Mother of God, commend me to thy Son
As here I bend;
And, oh, commend me when my task is done,
And life shall end.

A sinner kneeling at an Infant's cot
I call on Thee;
A sinner at the Cross forget me not,
But plead for me.
And thus in faith assured I leave my heart,
Blest Child with Thee;
A worthless gift with which Thou wilt not part
Eternally.

— *Author Unknown*

Stay with Me

Stay with me,
and then I shall begin
to shine as you shine,
so to shine as to be a light to others.
The light, O Jesus,
will be all from you.
It will be you who shines through me
upon others.
Give light to them as well as to me;
light them with me, through me.
Make me preach you without preaching—
not by words, but by my example
and by the sympathetic influence,
of what I do—by my visible resemblance
to your saints,
and the evident fullness
of the love which my heart bears to yours.

— *John Henry Newman*

The Almighty Word

While all things were in quiet silence,

and night was in the midst

of her swift course,

thine Almighty Word,

O Lord,

leaped down

out of thy royal throne,

alleluia.

— Author Unknown

Increase Our Faith

Lord, increase our faith.
We believe; help Thou our unbelief.
Give us a true child's trust in Thee,
in all Thy strength and goodness.
Cause us to rest in perfect confidence
in all Thy purposes and ways.
Enable us to confide all our interests
for time and for eternity
to Thy keeping.
Give us, heavenly Father,
the substance of things hoped for
and the evidence of things unseen,
that we may walk by faith,
not by sight,
looking not at the things
which are seen and temporal
but at those things
which are not seen and eternal.

— *Author Unknown*

Renaissance of Faith

Our Father,
remove from us the sophistication of our age
and the skepticism that has come, like frost,
to blight our faith and to make it weak.
Bring us back to a faith
that makes men great and strong,
a faith that enables us to love and to live,
the faith by which we are triumphant,
the faith by which alone
we can walk with Thee.

We pray for a return
of that simple faith,
that old-fashioned trust in God,
that made strong and great
the homes of our ancestors
who built this good land
and who in building left us our heritage.
In the strong name of Jesus,
our Lord, we make this prayer.

— *Peter Marshall*

PRAYERS OF WELCOME

For unto you is born this day in the city of David a Saviour, which is Christ the Lord. And this shall be a sign unto you; Ye shall find the babe wrapped in swaddling clothes, lying in a manger. And suddenly there was with the angel a multitude of the heavenly host praising God, and saying, Glory to God in the highest, and on earth peace, good will toward men. — Luke 2:11–14

PRAYERS OF WELCOME

Our Dear Lord

Our dear Lord and God,
your magnificent glory
comes to the world
through the humble birth
of your only Son.
We your people
have patiently prepared
for the coming of our Savior,
Jesus Christ,
and sing with joy
of the prophecy fulfilled.
May the darkness of night
be illumined by His glorious birth.
We pray that we may
carry this light of the world with us
throughout the year.
We ask this in your name. Amen.

— Author Unknown

Prayer for Christmas

Almighty God,
your eternal Word
pours down from heaven
as we wait in silence
this Christmas night.
We are filled with wonder
as we approach the manger
to welcome your Son.
Open our hearts to accept
and share His life.
Show us the gentle peace
and the true glory of the birth
of your Son. Amen.

— *Author Unknown*

Send the Light

Send, O God,

into the darkness of this troubled world,

the light of your Son:

let the star of your hope

touch the minds of all people

with the bright beams

of mercy and truth;

and so direct our steps that we may always walk

in the way revealed to us,

as the shepherds of Bethlehem

walked with joy to the manger

where he dwelt

who now and ever reigns in our hearts,

Jesus Christ our Lord.

— *John Wallace Suter*

A Christmas Hymn

The feast day of your birth resembles you, Lord.
Because it brings joy to all humanity.
Old people and infants alike enjoy your day.
Your day is celebrated from generation to generation.
Kings and emperors may pass away,
But you will be remembered till the end of time.
Your day is a means and a pledge of peace.
At your birth heaven and earth were reconciled,
Since you came from heaven to earth on that day
You forgave our sins and wiped away our guilt.
You gave us so many gifts on your birthday:
Spiritual light for those that are blind;
The cup of salvation for the thirsty;
The bread of life for the hungry.
In the winter when trees are bare,
You give us the most succulent spiritual fruit.
In the frost when the earth is barren,
You bring new hope to our souls.
In December when seeds are hidden in the soil,
The staff of life springs forth from the virgin womb.

— *Ephrem the Syrian*

Wilt Thou Help Us

Wilt Thou help each one of us
to keep Christmas alive in our hearts
and in our homes,
that it may continue to glow,
to shed its warmth, to speak its message
during the bleak days of winter . . .
May we hold to that spirit,
that we may be as gentle
and as kindly today
as we were on Christmas Eve,
as generous tomorrow
as we were on Christmas morning.

Before such mystery we kneel,
as we follow the shepherds and Wise Men
to bring Thee the gift of our love—
a love we confess has not always been
as warm or sincere or real
as it should have been.
But now, on this Christmas Day,
that love would find its Beloved,
and now from Thee receive the grace
to make it pure again, warm and real.

— *Peter Marshall*

The True Light

O God
who hast made
this most hallowed night resplendent
with the glory of the true Light;
grant that we
who have known the mysteries
of that Light on earth,
may enter into
the fullness of his joys in heaven.

— *Author Unknown*

Good Shepherd

Good Shepherd, thank You for
Your watchfulness through the night
and Your search for me
through days when I'm so lost
I forget that it's You I've found.
And when I've strayed from the fold,
give me the grace
to listen to Your voice,
to hear Your cry,
and to come running
to the One Who calls me,
among all His sheep,
by name.

— *Author Unknown*

Jesus, Newborn Child

Jesus, newborn child of all time,

We greet your birth with wide-eyed delight.

You are precious beyond words,

for our world

needs your presence more than ever.

Let the angels' promise of your good news,

offering joy and peace to all the world,

be heard by those who lead and guide.

Let kings bow down

and all creation greet this holy moment

as we seek to grasp its magnitude.

For you are God's gift

silently delivered to every human heart.

— *Author Unknown*

To the Christ Child

Teach, O teach us, holy Child,
By Thy face so meek and mild,
Teach us to resemble Thee,
In Thy sweet humility!

Hail, Thou ever-blessed morn!
Hail, redemption's happy dawn!
Sing through all Jerusalem,
Christ is born in Bethlehem.

— *Edward Caswall*

Child of Bethlehem

O sweet Child of Bethlehem,
grant that we may share
with all our hearts
in this profound mystery of Christmas.
Put into the hearts of men
this peace for which
they sometimes seek so desperately
and which you alone can give them.
Help them to know one another
better and to live as brothers,
children of the same Father.
Reveal to them also
your beauty, holiness and purity.
Awaken in their hearts
love and gratitude
for your infinite goodness.
Join them all together in your love.
And give us your heavenly peace.

— Pope John XXIII

What Shall We Offer?

What shall we offer thee, O Christ,
Who for our sakes
hast appeared on earth as man?
Every creature made by thee
offers thee thanks.
The angels offer thee a hymn;
The heavens a star;
The magi, gifts;
The shepherds, their wonder;
The earth, its cave;
The wilderness, the manger:
And we offer thee a virgin mother.
O God from everlasting,
have mercy upon us.

— *Author Unknown*

The Peace of Christ

O God, who centuries ago
blessed our earth with a vision
of thy love in the form of a little child;
who sent to rebuke earth's selfishness
a humble Man to go about doing good
and to speak the words of life;
who revealed thyself, the Conqueror of evil,
in one the weapons of whose warfare
were deeds of kindliness and mercy—
graciously grant us the Christmas
power as we remember him.
Fill our hearts with the gladness of his coming.
Teach us the enduring joy of his service.
Lead us into the Christmas peace
which passeth understanding,
the peace of Christ. Amen.

— *Morgan Phelps Noyes*

O God Our Father

O God our Father,
   who by the bright shining of a star
   led the wise men to the city of David:
   guide us by the light of your Spirit,
   that we too may come
   into the presence of Jesus
   and offer our gifts and our worship to him,
   our Savior and our Lord. Amen.

— *Alan Warren*

PRAYERS OF WELCOME

Now and Forever

Almighty God,
you make us glad with the yearly
remembrance of the birth
of your Son Jesus Christ.
Grant that as we joyfully receive him for our
redeemer, we may with sure confidence behold him
when he shall come to be our judge; who is alive
and reigns with you
and the Holy Spirit one God,
now and forever.

— *Author Unknown*

Praise of Heaven

Lord Jesus Christ,
Child of Bethlehem and Son of God:
help us this night to join our songs of glory
to those of the heavenly host,
that the joy of the church on earth
may be heard in the praise of heaven. Amen.

— C.N.R. Wallwork

PRAYERS OF BLESSING

For unto us a child is born, unto us a son is given:
and the government shall be upon his shoulder:
and his name shall be called Wonderful,
Counsellor, The mighty God, The everlasting
Father, The Prince of Peace.— Isaiah 9:6

Prayer for Our Home

God,
by your heavenly star,
you guided those who were wise
to your beloved Son, Jesus Christ.

May your blessing come to rest
on our home and all of us.
Make our lives
wise with your wisdom,
true to your teaching,
and enlivened by your love.
May your Word made flesh
make his home among us. Amen.

— *Author Unknown*

Thank You, Lord

Our Heavenly Father,
we ask Thy blessing upon all of us
this Christmastime.
Thank You, Lord,
that You had Yourself
born as a living mortal,
never to go away from us.
Help us so to draw near to You
that we may give ourselves
and be born in the name
of Jesus Christ our Lord. Amen.

— *Norman Vincent Peale*

A Prayer for Families

O God,
bless our family
and all its members and friends;
bind us together by your love.
Give us kindness and patience
to support each other;
and wisdom in all we do.
Let the gift of your peace
come into our hearts
and remain with us.
May we rejoice in your blessings
for all our days.
Amen.

— *Author Unknown*

Hope in His Promise

Lord our God,
the heavens are
the work of your hands,
the moon and the stars you made;
the earth and the sea, and every
living creature came into being
by your word. And all of us, too.
May this tree bring cheer to this house
through Jesus Christ your good and holy Son,
who brings life
and beauty to us
and to our world.
Lighting this tree, we hope in His promise.

— *Author Unknown*

The Christmas Spirit

Our God,

who hast mercifully and patiently

led us through the busy year,

give us at this Christmas time

the grace which was in Jesus Christ.

Let the spirit of the little child,

as it knocks today at the hearts of men,

enter our life and bless it.

Let duty become touched with delight,

and justice be forgotten in love.

Ofttimes we ask

that we may not fall short

of thy requirements.

Today we ask for more:

that obligation

may be changed to opportunity

and duty done with joy.

Ofttimes we ask that we may walk uprightly.

Today we pray for grace

to bow ourselves to others' needs.

Let our ears hear the cry of the needy,

and our hearts feel the love of the unlovely.
Give our hands strength
to do small things graciously.
Let our gifts today
be a privilege rather than a sacrifice
and let us accept kindness
with humility.
Heal the wounds of misunderstanding,
jealousy or regret,
and let the gentler air
of the Christmas spirit touch our lives,
as the cold of winter
is touched by the gentler days of spring.
As the old year ends
and the new year begins,
grant us peace with the world
and peace in our own hearts,
that those we love
and those whom we may help
may have sweet joy and rest. Amen.

— *Author Unknown*

We Thank You

Dear Lord,
we thank you today
for all these good things
to eat and drink,
and especially for those dear friends
and family members
who have come to be with us.
May the happiness we share together
on this Christmas day
shine in all our hearts forever.
Amen.

— *Author Unknown*

For This Day

For this day of the dear Christ's birth,
for its hours of home gladness
and world gladness,
for the love within these walls,
which binds us together as a family,
for our food on this table,
for our surroundings
in a land of freedom,
we bring to Thee, our Father,
our heartfelt gratitude.
Bless all these, Thy favors,
to our good, in Jesus' name.
Amen.

— *H.B. Milward*

A Christmas Blessing

May our Savior Jesus Christ
be with us wherever we go and in all that we do.
May the spirit of Christmas
warm our hearts all year long.
May the selfsame spirit of love
that bore our sins and led to our forgiveness
reside in us.
May we grow in the grace
and peace of the Child of Bethlehem.
Amen.

— *Author Unknown*

God Keep You

God keep you, dearest,
all this lonely night:
The winds are still,
The moon drops down
behind the western hill;
God keep you safely, dearest, till the light.

God keep you then
when slumber melts away,
And care and strife
Take up new arms
to fret our waking life,
God keep you through the battle of the day.

God keep you.
Nay, beloved soul, how vain,
How poor is prayer!
I can but say again, and yet again,
God keep you
every time and everywhere.

— Madeline Bridges

Bless Thy People

Our Heavenly Father,
we ask Thy blessing
upon all these, Thy people,
that we may see
and be wise enough
to follow the footprints
made by that little child
who has become our Saviour;
and that we may be great enough
in our minds and hearts
to walk in His footsteps
across the time that is allotted us
in this world.
Through Jesus Christ, our Lord.
Amen.

— *Norman Vincent Peale*

Uplift Our Hearts

Our Heavenly Father,
grant that Merry Christmas
may truly uplift our hearts.
Help us to give ourselves
to other people
and to have our hearts
filled with love
and our lives full of service
so that the Christmas spirit
will be in us all through the year.
Through Jesus Christ our Lord.
Amen.

— *Norman Vincent Peale*

A Christmas Prayer

O God our loving Father, help us
Rightly to remember the birth of Jesus,
that we may share in the song of the angels,
the gladness of the shepherds,
and the worship of the wise men.

Close the door of hate, and open
the door of love all over the world.
Deliver us from evil by the blessing
that Christ brings, and teach us
to be merry with clear hearts.

May the Christmas morning make us happy
to be Thy children and the Christmas
evening bring us to our beds with
grateful thoughts, forgiving and
forgiven, for Jesus' sake. Amen.

— *Robert Louis Stevenson*

A Season Blest

Give us, O Lord, a season blest
With quiet joys for Thy domain:
Let kindness calm the earth's unrest
And bring a peace to rough terrain.
Dispose of monetary powers
On land prolific with Thy seeds;
Bestow within the Yuletide hours
A unity of manmade creeds.

Like rain that permeates and soothes
Dry plains, saturate the nations.
Return the world to simple truths
Taught wisely by Thy Son of sons.
We hunger for Thee in our strife,
Become again the bread of life.

— *Betty Gardner Ackerlind*

PRAYERS OF PRAISE

Every day will I bless thee; and I will praise thy name for ever and ever. Great is the Lord, and greatly to be praised; and his greatness is unsearchable. — Psalm 145:2-3

O God of Love

O God, you are the object of my love,
Not for the hope of endless joys above,
Nor for the fear of endless pains below,
Which those who love you not must undergo.

For me and such as me, you once did bear
The ignominious cross, the nails, the spear:
A thorny crown transpierced your sacred brow;
What bloody sweats from every member flow.

Such as then was and is your love for me,
Such is and shall be still my love for thee;
Your love, O Jesus, will I ever sing—
O God of love, sweet Savior, dearest King!

— Saint Francis Xavier

This Is the Day

This is the day
which the Lord hath made:
let us rejoice and be glad in it.
For the beloved and most holy child
had been given to us
and born for us by the wayside
and hid in a manger
because there was no room in the inn.
Glory to God in the highest
and on earth peace to men of good will.
Amen.

— *Author Unknown*

All Praise to Thee

All praise to Thee, eternal Lord,
Clothed in a garb of flesh and blood;
Choosing a manger for Thy throne,
While worlds on worlds are Thine alone.

Once did the skies before Thee bow,
A Virgin's arms contain Thee now;
Angels, who did in Thee rejoice,
Now listen for Thine infant voice.

A little child, Thou art our guest,
That weary ones in Thee may rest;
Forlorn and lowly is Thy birth,
That we may rise to heaven from earth.

All this for us Thy love hath done,
By this to Thee our love is won,
For this we tune our cheerful lays,
And shout our thanks in ceaseless praise.

— *Martin Luther*

Fairest Lord Jesus

Fairest Lord Jesus,
Ruler of all nature,
O thou of God and man the Son!
Thee will I cherish,
Thee will I honor,
Thou, my soul's glory, joy, and crown.

Fair are the meadows,
Fairer still the woodlands,
Robed in the blooming garb of spring;
Jesus is fairer,
Jesus is purer,
Who makes the woeful heart to sing.

Fair is the sunshine,
Fairer still the moonlight
And all the twinkling, starry host;
Jesus shines brighter,
Jesus shines purer
Than all the angels heav'n can boast.

— *Author Unknown*

Shepherd of Youth

Shepherd of eager youth,
Guiding in love and truth
Through devious ways;
Christ, our triumphant King,
We come Thy name to sing,
And here our children bring,
To sound Thy praise.

Thou art our Holy Lord,
The all-subduing Word,
Healer of strife;
Thou didst Thyself abase,
That from sin's deep disgrace
Thou mightest save our race,
And give us life.

Ever be Thou our Guide,
Our Shepherd and our Pride,
Our Staff and Song;
Jesus, Thou Christ of God,
By Thy enduring word,
Lead us where Thou hast trod,
Make our faith strong.

— *Clement of Alexandria*

PRAYERS OF PRAISE

Jesu, Our Hope

Jesu, how sweet the memory
That fills my soul with thoughts of Thee!
But sweeter far Thou art to me,
When bowed before Thee tremblingly.

Never hath poesy been found
To utter word with sweeter sound
Than Thy dear name, sweet Jesu bound,
And pierced for us with many a wound!

Jesu, the hope of those who sigh,
Jesu, who hear'st the mourner's cry;
How good to those that to'ards thee fly,
But what to those who dwell on high!

Jesu, our only thought then be;
Jesu, our hope in misery;
Oh! may we soon, dissolved in Thee,
Thy praises sing eternally!

—J.J. Callanan

The Best Gift

Father, we thank you
for all your wonderful gifts to us.
Thank you for this special food.
Give us happiness
as we celebrate and share it together.
Thank you for your best gift of all–Jesus–
who came at this Christmas
season to bring us back to you.
Amen.

— *Author Unknown*

We Thank Thee

Our Heavenly Father,
help us open our hearts and minds
that Jesus may enter in.
We thank Thee for all
of the tender sentiment
of this wonderful day.
We thank Thee for our families,
our homes, our children,
and all that they mean to us.
What would we ever do without children?
Perhaps, Lord, You gave them to us
in order that we might ever have
the child mind and the child heart
and never part company
with wonder and excitement.
We thank Thee for our mothers and fathers,
our aunts, our uncles, our grandparents,
and all of the fellowship of the family.
Bind us together as with hoops of steel
and keep us in that fellowship
as long as earthly life shall last and beyond.

We gather as a greater family in Thy house,
at the feet of our Father—and of our Elder Brother
who has been given to us as the greatest gift of all,
even Jesus Christ.
May we be faithful throughout life,
and may He at last receive us to Himself
in Thy Heavenly Kingdom.
May we go out
from the experience of this Christmas
carrying Christmas in our hearts
and share the glad tidings
with our fellow men everywhere.
This prayer we pray
in the name of Jesus Christ our Lord.
Amen.

— *Norman Vincent Peale*

PRAYERS OF PRAISE

103

Light of the World

Jesus, Light of the world,
When I am afraid and unsure,
comfort me with the light of Your presence.
When loneliness chills me,
warm me with the light of Your love.
When the road ahead seems dark,
guide me with the light of Your way.
When I don't understand
and my thoughts are unclear,
fill me with the light of Your wisdom.
When I seem spent like a candle consumed,
replenish me with the light of Your life.
Then, so filled with Your light, use me,
so that I, with You,
may be a light for the world.

— *Father Wally Hyclak*

Hope of Glory

Almighty God, Father of all mercies,
we give thee most humble and hearty thanks
for all thy goodness and loving-kindness
to us, and to all men.
We bless thee for our creation,
preservation, and all the blessings of this life;
but above all, for thine inestimable love
in the redemption of the world
by our Lord Jesus Christ;
for the means of grace, and for the hope of glory.
And, we beseech thee,
give us that due sense of all thy mercies,
that our hearts may be unfeignedly thankful;
and that we show forth thy praise,
not only with our lips, but in our lives,
by giving up ourselves to thy service,
and by walking before thee in holiness
through Jesus Christ our Lord,
to whom, with thee and the Holy Ghost,
be all honour and glory, world without end. Amen.

— *Author Unknown*

Day after Christmas

O Lord Jesus,
we thank Thee
for the joys of this season,
for the divine love
that was shed abroad among men
when Thou didst first come as a little child...
Surely Christmas would teach us
the unforgettable lesson
of the things that matter most—
the ties that bind the structure of the family
upon which our country and all the world rests;
the love that we have for one another
which binds Thy whole creation
to Thy footstool, Thy throne...
So may Christmas linger with us,
even as Thou art beside us
the whole year through. Amen.

— *Peter Marshall*

Bless Our Home

Dear God: On this special day
when we celebrate the birth of Jesus,
we come together as a family
with thanksgiving and praise.
We praise you for the gift of salvation, and
we thank you for our family and friends.
Forgive us for all our sins,
and give us a forgiving heart
to forgive those who hurt us in the past.
May your Holy Spirit
reconcile and unite our family from this day forward.
We pray for each member of our family,
for your love and peace to surround us,
for your Holy Spirit to guide us,
for your loving arms to comfort us.
We pray for families who are suffering and in need.
Give us loving hearts to reach out to love them.
We dedicate this day to you.
We pray for your blessings upon our home.

— *Lia Icaza-Willetts*

A Prayer

Thou art not far from any one of us,
However far we are, O Lord, from Thee.
Give us the grace of quietness to know
Thy presence and Thy holy harmony
Within our hearts through all the hurried hours,
Through all the clamorous din of busy days,
Till in the listening silence of our souls
There stirs a song of worship and praise,
A song of praise to Thee for all Thy love,
A song of love for every living thing
That Thou, our Father and our God, hast made.
Oh, teach us to be still, that we may sing.

— Jane Merchant

The Gift

Heavenly Father,
Christmas began
with the gift of your Son
Who in turn gave the world
the gift of His life.
Let me remember, O God,
that Christmas remains
a matter of giving,
not parties, not presents,
not material wealth,
for Christmas is Christmas
When I give of myself.

— *Author Unknown*

Love

Heavenly Father,
in the pages of the Bible,
we can see the progress
of Mary and Joseph
as they journeyed
toward the most blessed event
in the history of the world.
Now, as once more we approach
the day of Your Son's birth,
help us to feel the holiness of this time.
Help us to honor the spirit
of Your wondrous gift
to us in Bethlehem: Love.

— *Author Unknown*

Author Index

Title Index